AF535096

MILLENARY

MILLENARY

poems by
Raeburn Miller

NO
PJ

A New Orleans Poetry Journal Press Book

Some of these poems have appeared in *Barataria Review*, *A Book of the Year* (Poetry Society of Texas), *Burning Deck*, *Cape Rock Journal*, *Counter/Measures*, *Epos*, *Integrity*, *The Lyric*, *Maple Leaf Rag*, (New Orleans Poetry Journal Press), *Midland* (Random House), *New Orleans Magazine*, *The New Orleans Review*, *PAPA: Publications of the Arkansas Philological Association*, *Poetry Northwest*, *Pontchartrain Review*, *The Southern Review*, and *Quicksilver.*

Special thanks are due to Richard Katrovas and Maxine Cassin, who made this book possible.

First Edition
M I L L E N A R Y

Library of Congress Catalog Card Number
85-063468

This project is jointly supported by a grant from the Louisiana State Arts Council through the Division of the Arts, Office of Cultural Development, Department of Culture, Recreation and Tourism, and the National Endowment for the Arts.

New Orleans Poetry Journal Press Books
2131 General Pershing Street
New Orleans, Louisiana 70115

for JRD and KNL

. . . who suggest me still . . .

CONTENTS

I.

Millenary, 11
The Longer Life, 12
Voices, 14
St. Bernard Avenue, 15
Tattoo, 16
Pro sua voluptate, 17
Luz, 18
Heat, 19
Unfound, 20
Death and the Hunky Number, 21
Menu Plan, 22
Words Without Thoughts, 23
A Translation from Memory, 24
Service, 25
Abstracts, 26

II.

New Job / First Poem, 39
Midas: 40
Medusa: 43
Another Oracle, 45
Signature, 46
Upon a Time, 47
The Damned Stream, 48
The Failed, 49
Begging Pardon, 50
The Patterned Chamber, 51
Winter Wasps, 52
What Happened, 53
Party, 54
Two for N.R.W., 55
A Moving Grave, 56

To Grow Old Is, 57
Heracles: 59

III.

Two Poems for Megan, 65
For a Student, 69
Assignation, 70
Luxe, calme, 71
Some Stanzas for Seraphia, 72
Chain Poem, 73
From a Stand-Up Routine, 74
Rereading an Early Poem, 75
Rite of Passage, 76
Serenade, 77
After the Visit, 78
Destination, 79
Admitting Absence, 80
On Some Movie Star Posters, 81
Science & Religion, 82
Facts About Roses, 83
As a Madman Slowly Cured Against His Will, 84
Conditions, 85
Shop Talk, 86
The Summing Up, 87
The Doe, 88

I

MILLENARY

> "a new terror...which shall
> brighten carefully these things"

The sun is an old terror.
We know it is wrong

to deduce from the eyeless denizens
of caves acquired characteristics—

yet who can help but feel
the eyes grow wider

the more we live in fear?
Carefully we come to see it all.

And like the eyes of the old
our sight grows dim, we who would

see dimly, who look elsewhere
—backward, inward—

and the new terror,
the familiar terror come again,

draws our faces to the east,
towards disclosure of this careful brightness.

THE LONGER LIFE

He contemplates suicide
to avoid contracting AIDS.

An earlier age
sinned to avoid more sin,

but Spenser's magniloquent
Despair descends to us

as self-reliance, nothing final.
Fathomed in time, unending

punishment holds one attraction:
that it should be unending.

A friend said of Dante's
downhill interest to her,

"The Purgatorio would be ok
if you didn't have to leave."

He knows more truth than he pretends,
but he contemplates suicide

for all the butch reasons.
He cannot face virtue,

potential virtue, potentiality
itself: he flounders in time

unable to escape
resurgent age, disease, the

piecemeal dying, piecemeal
salvation, being, the ragtag

hells afloat in God's care,
that fuel of all burning,

all quenching.

VOICES
(after Cavafy)

The abandoned artifacts of revered voices,
Left of lips dead now and underground
Or lips lost beneath the earth living—

They speak sometimes in our kinder sleep
Or come when the skillful mind lies pensive.

In their tones suddenly we hold, restored
For a tinge of presence, tunes of our first being,
Like faint nocturnal distances of music.

ST. BERNARD AVENUE

Around the streetlamps heavy mist.
Each leaf has collected one drop.
A high-crime neighborhood.

Not thinking of it, I take softer steps.
One light seems to move as I move,
A confusion of branches between us.

As if I would hide from you!
Would do violence to your care,
Or shake the brightness of you from the leaves!

TATTOO

is such a well
turned word—
I make
conversation at parties
about them when I
see them, and am
always caught up
in those same details
whether followed by
pride or regret
or curiously both, a
onetime sailor's half-
dramatic sense of
the flesh and what it leaves us.

PRO SUA VOLUPTATE

If time exists only in the mind,
procreation exists in the mind.

The dandelions of the field
indeed sow, lie down in tatters,

and every wife of Solomon
was a virgin once,

every queen makes much of time.
Let us grow old together

we say to ourself,
there will be no one else at last

to close our eyes. Now when we close
our eyes, we see the instant, opening

its flower, its fragile flower.
It is life, it is birth, it is momentary,

this amplitude of sterile love.

LUZ

Do not search for the North Pole.
God, who is everywhere,
especially in barren places,

lives especially where great ice
thrusts and groans all the year round.
Do not fly over the mountains

where there are year-long snows.
Love God where he is least.
In the cities where none stand firm,

search there, among whatnots,
men, slabs, banners.
We are warm creatures,

what passes through our veins
is life itself, and we may look
within for what we have not found—

the antipodes forever, God's presence,
who is elsewhere as well,
in the zero of the absolute.

HEAT

Northerners warm their hands,
Southerners their rear ends.
Cold hands, you know, warm heart.
But it's down yonder spends

Heat from the heart, attests
To its safety, to its harm.
All lovers go bare-assed.
Though this March day is warm

And I housed close, I take
No chances with desire—
My hands behind my back,
I back up to the fire.

UNFOUND

The head of a hanged man feels the weight of his body. In death they work against each other, and in life.

The head is a double agent. And there is truth as deep as the blood.

How should we die? Decisively.

I stretch out my hand like a scaffold.

The hanged man sees his life, his guilt. The hanged man sees his innocence. He looks down from his height.

He tries, but his feet cannot reach the ground.

His head dies, his dead body is his own, his oneness has broken him.

DEATH AND THE HUNKY NUMBER

Lion's tooth and lion's claw.
Animals with jawbones.
Defense perimeters.

My lips are cut
from passion—a violence
important, casual,

like to die.
A dream caravan
drawn by lions.

Along the horizon
marchers on water
stalk. My blood

seeps under my tongue,
impenetrable
as black sea,

the claws of the dolphin,
the fangs of the gull.
And death a hard-on

battering my face in.

MENU PLAN

"A la carte is the way to his heart." —John Delaney

I am going to go have fun.
It will pierce me.

I am going to hang around.
And I'm not picky.

Wow! Wow! What a dog!
And yet you never know.

I have been as hungry as a man.
I could have eaten a full meal.

I am famished still but for nothing.
Prophecy is a crumb too small to bite.

Show me someone lovely
and I'll make love.

Show me anyone
and I'll make do.

I am desperate, I am lost,
I am alone, I am dying, I am sinful,
I am waiting for dessert.

WORDS WITHOUT THOUGHTS

I should be more grateful than I am.
Yet any grace is spectacular.

Tightrope walkers take their time.
And musicians and court reporters.

Like a rooster in the frail light,
No man can come to terms with his monotony.

A healthy cripple knows himself.
My love is like my love's body.

Antique cars and Confederate money
Grow precious for their worthlessness.

At the moment I am thin.
His cancer has withdrawn from him right now.

And God is graceful, like a dancer.
I pray in a kind of applause.

If God could accept time as a gift,
If only God could accept time as a gift—

What is it I want? Why, to be grateful.
My hands cover my face like a clock.

A TRANSLATION FROM MEMORY
(Baudelaire)

That servant you were jealous of,
We ought to take her a few flowers—
The dead themselves have heavy sorrows.
I dreamed last night she stood above
Our coupling and would have cried out
From that mouth too far gone for sound.
When you beneath me quicken breath
Let lust unite our thoughts of death,
Let your dark eyes widen and close
To know she still may watch us there
Through those blank sockets where her tears
Last night, all for our sake, arose.

SERVICE

The ping and pong of tower chimes
Measure the mass that others keep.
I lie in bed and mingle rhymes,
A plushy sinner half asleep.

On other couches lovers strive
To mend their vow, or houseled limbs
In cramp and sweat hold out alive.
I thumb a book of synonyms.

In seven days the world was said,
They say. God is more deft than I,
Who snuggle in my Sunday bed
To masturbate and versify.

ABSTRACTS

1

Must they hold back and break my heart,
These phantoms trembling like a desert?
I looked to them for water.
I went on, not after them.
It is hopeless now. It is a long journey.

2

My sins were once gluttony and lust gone astray.
I still suffer from those deaths, but less
Since long sloth has held me down
The way I would weigh more on a heavier planet.
Now despair, like a passerby at night
Indistinct, could motion toward distraction,
Toward danger, or gradually recede
Meaningless too into pale distance.

3

They say the accidents of a whole life fall together at the end
Into substance or even beauty.
I have looked toward that conclusion, but now I am tired.
Now I want to see more from here.
I could believe the moments of my life
Move burning together as I journey from them
And apart as I approach.
I could believe, given a place to look from,
That the moments of my life are blue and red with meaning.
Yes, I want to make something of myself,
I want to be substantial now,
I want to get my bearings toward some fixed Vega.

4

I have done all I can for right now
But the moment is not enough.
In spite of myself, I believe change matters.
I take on the way, like a burden.
I carry the journey along the journey.
Christ, who bore the cross to be borne by it,
Where did you go? where did you go?
I know you turned a moment on your way
To weep for the stones of the city,
To weep for some women standing there.

5

I am in love again and again I am silent.
I am afraid of saying something wrong,
Of doing harm to myself or others through love.
I sit out late listening to passing sounds,
And to love, which comes like singing from a chapel
    across fields,
Like the singing of sisters who have no wish to entertain,
Who sing to celebrate a kingdom that is within themselves.

6

God is a great wheel, a returning.
Sometimes a drunken joke is still funny later—
When I said my mother used to eat dog food,
He answered, Son of a gun.
We cut a foolish figure, tilting with God.
My love has breasts like a woman.

7

Art lives because we accept it.
You say it all happened before I came.
I know better, I know the looks, I know
What it means to give up craft, shoulder your hasseling.
It means starting over, making it new.
I am only safe
As oyster shells crushed into the roadbed,
I am only safe as broken windows
After the glass is put back.

8

I know a tall man who loves a great Dane.
When I try to hurt him, he won't listen,
Yet the fool thinks that I could be his friend.
In the wilderness, in the hermit's cave
Where salamanders burn on the sand and the saint
Sitting alone is his own fire—
There a man can struggle at loving God,
The grand emasculation, the burning blood
Gushing like sunlight from the slashed God.
But here there are the others, nearer.
I reach my hand, I love what I can hurt.
My true love is growing his beard.

9

In the dark woods at night
When most beasts are quieter,
Most birds sunk upon a sway of branches,
The bats from their caverns swoop and eat,
The dark their furniture, their thoroughfare.
I too am sinful. I lie awake listening.
Sometimes I feel as though I too
By screaming could find where I am.

10

The dark way, the desert journey—
I keep seeing that still landscape.
Love rising like waves of heat in the distance,
Like the shrine of Zeus Ammon such a long way
Through darkness to find a father, like three kings
Through darkness to find a new god—
Completed to be repeated, the ancient passage.
Night and silence. I keep saying that.

II

NEW JOB / FIRST POEM

My desk cleared awhile
of unfamiliar paperwork,
I lean back,

open myself to distance,
and see the Prodigal Son
penniless at the sties.

The image puzzles me—
I who am more nearly
elder brother, father,

slopped shoat.
Now he looks up, as if
he too sought to imagine

meaning, as if indeed
he knew my name from a parable
and felt no surprise

to see me there,
to see me here.

MIDAS:

Don't say I never warned you
affluence brings with it
environmental pollution—

but keep the gold.
Recently I have spent
my royal highness

counting calories
while a good stereo
plays in the background

semi-classical selections.
Such is the stillness
of a king's poverty.

Go ahead and laugh.
Remember, though,
I once knew gods

and could have fingered you
to gravity forever.
That's done now—

but how you would have gleamed!
I remember those days—
panic, joy,

that heavy wealth.
The lead pencils gold, the lampcord,
my cat a burden on my knees,

its fur still fluffy,
all gold, the *TV Guide*,
the toothbrush bristles,

pennies and dimes turned gold,
gold cufflinks real gold,
ping pong balls, Kleenex

crumpled and dropped, ice cream,
storefront glass gone dark,
the mist of gold

blowing off me in a breeze,
such tangible glory!
Certainly I starved,

certainly I mourned—
at a loss to save
my life for such grandeur.

I couldn't manage.
Yet hungry as I was,
I stood a long time

staring down a long time
at those pale sands
where I had washed

my gift away.
Now this rest of me
softens toward death,

empty-handed.
When my father died
he tied a knot,

an intricate legacy
for someone else,
all of Asia.

Not for me—
my ambitions are over,
a memory of brightness

beyond my grasp,
a shimmer, a ripple,
a hearkening of gold.

MEDUSA:

My halls and garden
are full of statues.
Seeing them one might think

my tastes Hellenistic,
Victorian perhaps,
so accurate the detail,

so consistent the expression
of polite inquiry,
with only occasionally

a shadow like surprise
or the approach of horror.
No, I would have preferred

Brancusi or pre-Columbian,
or better still
something classical,

calm, heroic, unadorned,
naked even.
So many costumes!

When I move among them,
these cold men and women
stare at me.

Stone has that right,
yet I find it strangely hard
to meet their eyes.

Their stillness oppresses
till I long for company,
not this limestone postman,

this iron deer.
It is as if
I were the visitor

and these unyielding lords
had summoned me
in blank condescension

that I should walk the aisles
of their estate
to distract them from weariness.

ANOTHER ORACLE

When finally I kill
My father, it shall be
In the close act of love,
As he brought death to me.

The lumbering of my heart,
The wheeze that knots my breast—
From him each final part
That falters into rest.

Thus I go mortal on
But wage, towards his defeat,
A quarrel in the groin,
The place where three roads meet.

SIGNATURE

Black ink outlasts blue or
so the archivist decrees, and
so for years to come black ink
will unintelligibly be in-
sisted upon upon those documents in
such a Latinate configuration, such
occult flourishes of papers meant to be un-
folded only in the dark.

A black and blue mark on the
neck, left there by a lover's
kiss or rather by the kiss of
one one pretends was a lover
who was only one making love
and gone, will not last.

UPON A TIME

Every ever after is happy—
nonexistent, naturally, but

gladly so. The present is the pea
the princess lies awake upon,

her wakefulness is salvation,
but how tired she is, never

knowing what it means, never
to wake who cannot sleep.

That which is has not been and cannot
come to be, yet she stretches in discomfort—

and I am going to have been
alive, which is as much as one may rest on,

I have done it all from start to scratch.

THE DAMNED STREAM

The past, like the future
neither known nor unknown,

is nothing to fear.
How many things we fear

are nothing to fear!
My dreams are full of old sins.

Yet daily I maraud
for food and bodies,

fearing nothing—
I who should cower at what is,

this known, this knowable,
this present driven through me like a stake—

who fear instead
sleep, memory, imaginary judgment,

harmless elsewheres inhabited
by no living soul.

THE FAILED

We exclude from our accounts of history
all that is not our own.

The past, of course, is not our own.
Even memory—that soft embankment—

even memory is here and now.
History, for all its self-assurance, sticks close.

We look out the window
at a brick wall,

we tell tales of that magic vista—
the passersby as featureless as air.

And when my hand reaches out
as far as I can reach,

it brushes the fingers of my other hand
reaching out.

BEGGING PARDON

They do not listen to me anymore.
Secretaries, strangers on street corners,
telephone solicitors, friends, lovers,
they all interrupt the wanderings of my sentence
and answer something that I never said.

God himself does not wait for my amen.

Now in my reverie my impatient self
Opens my shirt cuff and my white wrist.

THE PATTERNED CHAMBER
(after Li Shang-yin)

This inexplicable lute has fifty strings.
I twist its slackened pegs and remember time.
The Red King slept while the notes fluttered away,
And Philomela faltered at the sound of blood.
The moon and the pearl are one, the eye and its sea,
But here the city sky is distant jade.
All remoteness is as sudden as meeting again.
Meeting again is as final as this broken music.

WINTER WASPS

Trapped in the pane, these wasps
Make do with death. They fall
In one late lovers' clasp
And break and feel the cold.

Neither outside nor in
Their thin wings could outlast
The narrowing of the light
Against the chill northwest.

They chose a middle reach
Encased by glass and dust
Where their brief season beats
Its quick, exhausting lust.

WHAT HAPPENED

The fashion for Dylan Thomas among clerics
Is hard to understand. The scientific method
Is useful as a tool of social oganization.
Dinner party conversation, whether about
People, events, or abstract ideas,
Can be boring, stands a demonstrable chance
Of being boring, so that what interests us
Must not be substance, must be style,
A truth God must surely know, or say an opinion
God must hold, an observation God must
Have made, a conclusion God must have drawn.

PARTY

"With my necktie by my ear, I was stepping on my dear"

I stepped on her foot, on her
kneecap, I stepped on her left
breast, I stepped on her soft
palate, on her fingers one by
one, on her retina, on
auricles, ventricles, bronchi,
I stepped on my dear
deliberately, with care, with
great concern, I stepped on
her hair.

The necktie reminded me
of where I was, the necktie
swung me off her and
it was like I was going
to die.

TWO FOR N.R.W.

I.

I touched him and within a day he died.
She mocks that I have not cut short her breath.
What I could say would hurt mine and her pride:
Such, Love, is the consistency of death.

II. (Seven years later)

My touch took longer this round, but it felled.
You were indeed proud, now indeed are dead,
That bantering life dispatched from what I held
To have the last word when the verse is read.

A MOVING GRAVE

His eyes are dimming, he who has
so moved on, prospered.
For what honey should he still

yearn, from what carcass?
He understands, as only
a conscience in chains could, God's

seriousness, the to-do of
tresses, flow charts. He
accepts his losses, his receding

forehead, a bulk never to be
strong again nor see it all.
Philistines worship their

figurative and pliant images,
in the ranks of whom he labors
at a desk for slaves.

TO GROW OLD IS

To grow old is
to question time's meaning—

not greedily
as we question youth,

fame, all we lost hope for,
but, well, wisely?

Let it be so.
When I put my fingers in hot water

the veins on the back of my hand
swell twice their size.

Does time engorge time?
We were and are ourselves,

yet every day
(and day is a giveaway)

we are another's palpitation,
a different face,

blue, distorted.
We liken time to distance

saying that the vista rises
and grows faint.

Westward, we say, posturing—
another metaphor, another lie.

Space is solid,
unquestionable—

at least we do not lose our faith
in this corner, that obliquity,

as our frame misshapes us.
We lose faith in time.

And it is faith we search for.
We could bear up under its certainty.

The refractions of the hour
are what betray us.

We look into the expanse
and cannot keep it,

cannot count it,
cannot match its pieces,

we shudder as we did not once,
when twice was once again.

HERACLES:

The hind that I follow
is a doe with antlers,
and those antlers are gold.

Strange quarry! I have fought
many monsters
but this opponent

offers no challenge
but elusive flight,
the exhaustion of loss—

not loss even,
only hard patience,
breathless, unceasing.

Sometimes I run
mile after mile
without reassurance

to point the horizon
she vanished toward
or to give warning

if her speed has stood hidden
as I pressed by.
Sometimes I find

white slashed on gray
where her bronze hoof
struck fire from stone,

or a web of her hair
like dark sunlight
against tree bark.

A few times I have fancied
beyond a clearing
the gold of far antlers

among green branches.
Then she was gone
and I gone after.

Long ago
she was consecrated–
a virgin's offering–

to that calm Goddess
who with her bow
cares for the frightened,

but I mean no harm
and this hind's fleetness
is skill, not fear.

I pause a moment:
it's been a long way
and the doe runs lightly.

Sometimes I think
I shall never take her,–
she is a thin dream,

a lie in the heart,
the gold of her horns
fool's gold,

like the color of light
broken on water.
That despair

is the true labor.
But now I run on,
the landscape before me

rising and falling.
Faint in the distance now
a pulse of hoofbeats,

a tumbling in the underbrush,
a flicker of gold flame
leaping and gone.

III

TWO POEMS FOR MEGAN

I.

You do not know enough to know that weather
Is unpredictable, but has no will of its own,
That when last night was eighteen below zero
No harm was meant. You are so safe, unborn,
That I think of you mostly in terms of self-pity,
Saying, Ah, she must come breathe-in the same cankered air
That here rusts my lung, poor innocent, must learn to feel
Her cheeks and forehead tighten numb the first clear night
After snow, only to burn and swell when she arrives home.
And yet I know that where you are, that tangible landscape
Of shelter from the night air and the ubiquitous snows,
Is no where for endurance, for a satisfactory translation of
unknowns
Into substantial flakes and encounters, that to remain where
you are
Would be ultimate coldness, your flesh frozen into the cramp
Of sense without the patterning touches of imagination,
That only by unclenching your fist from the warm cordage
And fighting out into alien weather can you hope to achieve
The open porch still beyond passage.
Once here, and despite all our further protests
Of more self-pity that you shall enter the storm
Of death in seldom summer and disaffection,
You must weave your mind toward its perceptible sequence,
Determined to accept your final exposure
As an unsounded reassurance of purpose enough.
And this mindless weather will be your doing, the white snow
Your satisfactory warmth of a larger safety,
And once more you must escape, but this time, kicking free
Of the constricting sky, you will arrive at a wider exile,
And the body you are piecing together now and the
mind's delicate emotions
That you will master in your journey of climate and trouble

Will yield their assertiveness to the breath's luminous demands,
And both the red darkness and the uninformative sky
Will have opened into a true expanse of completeness
    without demarcation
Where blood is Christmas ribbon and the snow falls
For your sake beautifully of its own accord.

II.

One day old and you have already learned
How to glance aside to see your tears' effect
Through glass on our unknown faces. You are stubborn,
I decide, but coy. I go back to your mother.

    Last night I thought a long time about love,
    How any choice is mostly a denial,
    Even holding hands, how there is no way out
    But holding hands — or else going in the kitchen
    To lean your head against the wall a moment,
    Wanting tears, but no outside comfort. And either path
    Is a narrowing of the horizon, a descent.

A couple of times this morning I slipped and called you
My nephew, but then I hadn't see you cry
With such obvious delight in your own noise
That you had to stop occasionally to chuckle.
I am not likely to forget now you are a woman.
But until you have grown awhile and been hurt,
Your pleasure in tears is too simple. It frightens me.
I go back gladly to your intricate mother.

    Holding hands can be a satisfaction
    Like having the whole apartment to oneself
    Can be a satisfaction. Neither lasts.
    Hands part to light another cigarette
    And beautiful faces in a theatre lobby
    Reappear on the refrigerator door
    Or over the sprawled pages of a fallen book.

Yet be coy, my dear, and cry. It will get you far,
Though not far enough. But if you learn
Truly skillful tears and to open your eyes,
You need never want for salads and cosmetics.
I know one who once needed such things
And gathered them from air, who is now a mother.

I know what it is like to fear summer
And the lost touch of separated hands
Or to think of getting supper alone at sixty
With an unwashed fork and too much grease, on
a tabletop
Stacked with newspapers and catalogues.
And I know what it is like not to decide,
To wait at night for one trustworthy hint
Past thirty and past forty and past waiting.

You will learn that pearls are lovelier than oysters,
Poems than poets, how to choose stationery,
When to change the subject. And you will be unhappy.
And that is the time to learn another crying,
Silent and dry inside from the long fear
Of knowing and enduring what is yours
Here and no more and inescapable.
That birth-pains should go hard through all Easter
Reminds us, yet is only one granite shiver
From the quarried slope where nothing grows except
The prospect of superior distance, where I have seen
Your mother climbing in the thin sunlight.

To be alone or not be alone
Or not to be. And our choices are made for us.
It is vain to sweat and calculate at night
Looking for theories in the tangled stars;
And whether at last the hands slacken, or never
Never have touched, what is important for our life
Is not the given stone but the long carving
To jewelry sets or garden walls or grave markers.

You were born from two who are in love, who live
Hand in hand, and I, who sulk in a corner
And fidget and complain and eat cake,
Should not instruct you in how and when to cry.
But it does seem certain that pain ultimately
Is the secret, and I would have you grow at last
Beyond mere coyness into knowledge. For that time
I entrust you to your mother and to Our Mother.

And Our Mother of Good Counsel, pray for us.
Empty into our cradled narrow bed
The stubborn light that rushes from your palms
To steal an apple and a rose for love.
Give us our weariness and indecision,
Give us our pain. And help us learn to cry
In coy, genuine tears as winningly
And glance as simply as a one day girl
Beyond the pane to where all choice is home.

FOR A STUDENT

My love for you is my best love:
This no denials can harm, nor hands,
Nor change, which none is master of,
Nor chance, which no one understands.

At conscious moments I may bend
Quickened with fancied innocence,
But conscience towards my better end
Cites me the sources for pretense.

I draw back like a frosty sage
To read sweet nothings line by line
And mark your errors down the page
As red as any valentine.

ASSIGNATION

I turn the television off
And wait for silence to close in.
Then darkly and alone I fall
To fugitive and cloistered sin.

My toothpaste and deodorant needs—
Consuming passions!—are the same
As for my fellow average men,
Or so the intimate ads proclaim.

But late at night I can break free
To grit my yellow teeth and sweat,
Alone in my one perfect love
Beyond good manners or regret.

LUXE, CALME

Set the prayerwheel where the fresh stream can turn it.
Let your tongue rest from God, let your hands rest.
Love is a burden hour by hour by hour.
Come sink your cool head on my careless breast.

Our eyes have rolled from earth to heaven and closed.
Our throats have swallowed flesh and spat up words.
Our cocks have knelt and spilled life on the ground.
Our minds have dimmed their songs like covered birds.

God waits in clockwork, clicking at mere this
That is no love—but let what else be later.
Tomorrow you may save yourself for death.
Let us float now like tired swimmers in water.

SOME STANZAS FOR SERAPHIA

I. Our only heroes, heroines;
Our dramas softened into novels.
At coffee we discuss discuss
How Don grew sad last night at Lucy's—
When he denied it, whether he knew.
No Vikings plunge west on these shallows,
No thongs resolve these knotted hands.

II. Those we lived with in what seemed kindness
Have fallen away to alcohol
Or shock treatment in parish wards.
We rent our downstairs rooms to strangers,
Though ours the expenses of repair:
I dreamed once that my once true love
Had slashed himself with a can opener.

III. I'm swirled profane through those black rapids,
The falling currents of your hair;
But foundered at ten past the hour,
I go to shuffle paper sails
And you to wizard coves of telling
Your tears' full tally of depressions.
Our martyrdom is to grow old.

IV. For us beyond the Matterhorn
No plain of mauve and olive distance.
We wander through the labyrinth
To find quiet death—no Minotaur
Ramps down the echoes of our maze.
Thread back these lines until you reach
My footsteps tangled at the end.

CHAIN POEM

Strapped language—
words are masochists.

George went to Texas for sex.

Language is an alarm
triggered by the cat.

What I have to say
is no friend.

I must be kind to be cruel.

Any journey is long.
Any sex is heartless.

Twist a sentence and beat me.

FROM A STAND-UP ROUTINE

How does a porcupine make love?
With stricter care than you and I,
Who clutch abandoned, drawing blood,
And, mutually defended, die.

REREADING AN EARLY POEM

It was the old subject.
Time clashing on contemplation.
Sex banging love.

We are old enough now
to make enemies.

I am a man
I hate to see cry.

I look back on myself
like a clock turned to the wall.

I look back on God
like a sunflower
shadowing a sundial.

Whoever wrote all that
died and went to heaven.
Let his poem pray.

Let his words and meditations
be acceptable in my sight.

My eyes water. The mind
slackens before the body.

All those poets lied—
no, guessed young.

Me too. It's a let down,
these verses about love.

I pray to be as true
now as then
it felt to say so.

RITE OF PASSAGE

"the body, delighting in thresholds" —Roethke

A man pushes a wheelbarrow through a gate.
A stone god falls broken before the ark.

Sex, he said, stretching,
is a substitute for sex.

We feel pain differently,
conditioned by experience, temperature, pride.

The gallery, the courtyard,
the open road that winds away,

the gatekeeper, the signpost—
over what threshold does the rain

sweep with such insistence,
with the body's love?

As if the pulse could account for our condition,
as if we went on from here,

as if the heaped barrow might hold the secret of harvest,
of seed grain made golden perhaps by sacrifice.

SERENADE

Is the moonlight expensive?
Yes and no.

Reflect on the earth,
heavy and turning.

Ponderous and impending,
the earth suffers like gold.

How does gold suffer?
Incorruptibly.

Pay for the moon
by turning your face away.

Rustic, bloody, dear—
and common as darkness.

I count the cost and hold you.
I tilt my watch to the moon.

AFTER THE VISIT

A man's reach
must, well, you
are gone back now,
exceed, and I
must say good
morning Jim, good
morning Shirley, good
morning again and
again and I am
stuck now, good
morning, his grasp,
something about
"our mutual flame"
oh shit!—but it
is true, I do
stiffen like a
rusted motor
frozen with fire.

DESTINATION

"It's sea-level for us from now on." —Vern Rutsala

Flat, that's what.
Every shape's another horizon.
Bodies curve like distance.

We run down like waves.
Tugged here, tugged there,
no more climbing.

Even this dead end
is still downhill,
falling over ourselves.

We who played like fountains,
who cared nothing for the truth,
we are on the level.

The sea pants like a fallen runner.
From now on we lie where we fall.
Have fallen so often and have fallen.

ADMITTING ABSENCE

Yes, sex is overrated—
but it's all we've got.

Art is clumsy,
religion paradoxical,
food comes to a bad end.

And I asked how flowers
can overweight their stems,
break them, dangle—

flowers whose aim is lust,
that shrunken seed.
You blamed the rain.

I think of you in Denver.
I shake it off and make a sandwich.
I open Li Po.

Two friends part and their horses neigh.
Down the high vault your contrails scrawl a long sigh.

ON SOME MOVIE STAR POSTERS

Bigger, my loves, than life
You look down from the wall
Without batting an eye
As if ripeness were all.

But James Dean is long gone
And Garbo has grown old
With being left alone
And Mae West lies down cold.

Black and white, paper, flat,
Hang on as best you may,
Calm as the sky at night
Whose shining is decay.

SCIENCE & RELIGION

"The cloister and observatory saint
take comfort," ah yes,

let 'em complain.
When a star falls,

after all,
it burns down always,

almost. It's small,
it's dark again forever.

And the cloister?
Well, let those saints be light

if that's their will.
Let the equivocal holiness

that burns in solitude
make one our destined

observance. We are
worms, of course, glowing.

FACTS ABOUT ROSES

I repeat so often these days, My love is like
A red red rose, aimlessly, at street corners
When the engine dies, or in bed at night
After the final television program,
The convenient and untroubled prayer, and the
  national anthem,
Have blanked into a splatter of dancing flashes
With nothing comprehensible left to say,
And I say, aimlessly, scarcely noticing,
My love is like a red red rose, my love
Is like, is like—and I remember love
In colorless dreams of wax or plastic flowers,
And then I begin the motor, if I can,
And drive on.
                    I know two facts about roses:
That one poet saw their petals arranged like saints
And another as the symbol of the unit.
Mathematicians tell me that one is one
And the lily-white boys in green that one is one
And I brood on age, reciting scraps of poems.

I have walked through the tall graves of New Orleans
Looking for backgrounds for still photographs
And watched bouquets sweat in their turn toward death,
Brown, slow. I have thought of scenes in novels,
Lovers strolling through flowers, my love is like
A whole basket of freshly cut roses
Twisted from colored paper in Japan.

And may the one God move in my carburetor
And may his angels temper my just dreams.
Integrity is like a red, red rose,
For which I offer my undivided attention
Driving backwards and forwards, 1200 miles away,
Waking, eating, reciting, falling asleep.

AS A MADMAN SLOWLY CURED AGAINST HIS WILL

As a madman slowly cured against his will
Feels a deep compromise burning like shame
Behind the sophistries of his outward joy,
I lift up my hand and watch it in the light
Saying, "Now it will surely show through the simple skin,
The blood is so sharp, the task of flesh so tender."

My hand betrays nothing. It turns steadily
Like a tool. All bodies are geared for deceit.
But now in dreams my sinister hand bleeds,
Mopping my forehead's sweat to red frowns,
A brow in danger. In dreams the knife slits
Persecution away: the greater persecution.

Waking I lie as still and great as China.
I have done no wrong except in doing right.
If my hand is clean, why need I ask its judgment?
They were bad, the lonely visions, a child's conceit.
But at good-night, what may I better remember?
In the grave awake, and life a landslide of dream?

CONDITIONS

I have heard it said
that in the land of
the dead it is not
necessary to
go to bed when you
want to make love right.
Instead, you make love
all over all the
time the way the sun
above shines, which sounds
stunning, but still I
dread the thought of how
tired one must be and
how strong to remain
faithful and to keep
on, uncomforted,
even when there is
no breathing, nothing
ahead, no going
afterwards to sleep.

SHOP TALK

My office window fronts the lake.
Long hours of water looking prove
Incentive for no toil beyond
The usual heart's demand for love—

A love as whole as Pontchartrain,
As interrupted by whitecaps,
As indistinct along the sky,
As round and small on public maps.

Desire is simple, looking out—
But at my back old drouth prevails:
A desk of cluttered paperwork
In folds of white like fallen sails.

THE SUMMING UP

I cannot believe I am unimportant—
a failure, of course,

but such an important failure.
When I say it has been in vain

I speak with such grace,
posturing my splendid vanity.

My sowings wait somewhere,
broadcast, faithful, beyond stone—

some archivist will unfold me
shuddering under my light.

Surely such nothing could not come to nothing.
I buck up,

I start to cook supper,
I look forward to stacking the clean dishes on the shelf.

THE DOE

"Her work, whate're it be, is done."

She sleeps on the ground on Sundays
and thus her work is done,

has been long done. I sleep
too, I too sleep like suffering,

where I fall, but my work
is not done, is scarcely

begun. Whatever my work is.
Time works hard, never still,

filling every rift with the
sweat of someone else's brow.

All white things speak of grace,
are passive, all things know

whatever work was worth doing
was done long ago, in seven

days perhaps, perhaps in six,
six billion years, whatever

time that was, whatever whiteness,
whatever work it could have been.

We lie beside a grave.